I0201649

WORLDVIEW GUIDE

THE STRANGE CASE

OF DR. JEKYLL & MR. HYDE

Ben Palpant

canonpress
Moscow, Idaho

Published by Canon Press
P.O. Box 8729, Moscow, Idaho 83843
800.488.2034 | www.canonpress.com

Ben Palpant, *Worldview Guide for Dr. Jekyll & Mr. Hyde*
Copyright ©2017 by Ben Palpant.
Cited page numbers come from the Canon Classics edition (2017), www.canon-press.com/books/canon-classics.

Cover design by James Engerbretson
Cover illustration by Forrest Dickison
Interior design by Valerie Anne Bost and James Engerbretson

Printed in the United States of America.

All rights reserved. No part of this publication may be reproduced, stored in a retrieval system, or transmitted in any form by any means, electronic, mechanical, photocopy, recording, or otherwise, without prior permission of the author, except as provided by USA copyright law.

Unless otherwise indicated, Scripture quotations are from the NKJV® Bible, copyright © 1982 by Thomas Nelson. Used by permission. All rights reserved.

A free end-of-book test and answer key are available for download at www.canonpress.com/ClassicsQuizzes

Palpant, Ben, author.
Dr. Jekyll and Mr. Hyde worldview guide / Ben Palpant.
Moscow, Idaho : Canon Press, [2017].
LCCN 2019011335 | ISBN 159128242X (paperback : alk. paper)
LCSH: Stevenson, Robert Louis, 1850-1894. Strange case of Dr. Jekyll and Mr. Hyde.
LCC PR5485 .P35 2017 | DDC 823/.8--dc23
LC record available at https://lccn.loc.gov/2019011335

17 18 19 20 21 22   9 8 7 6 5 4 3 2 1

CONTENTS

INTRODUCTION

Robert Louis Stevenson wrote several celebrated stories, including *Treasure Island* and *Kidnapped*, but *The Strange Case of Dr. Jekyll and Mr. Hyde* is his best-selling work. Forty-thousand copies sold within the first six months of publication. In this novella, London lawyer Gabriel Utterson uncovers a strange and startling connection between his friend, the respectable doctor Henry Jekyll, and the sinister Edward Hyde. *Dr. Jekyll and Mr. Hyde* is an arresting portrait of one man's struggle with the human condition.

THE WORLD AROUND

The Strange Case of Dr. Jekyll and Mr. Hyde was first published in January of 1886. In that year, the Statue of Liberty—the symbol of freedom found in America—was dedicated, the last major US-Indian war ended when Apache Chief Geronimo surrendered, Karl Benz built and drove the first automobile, and Sigmund Freud opened his practice in Vienna. The 1880s marked the second industrial revolution and a major shift in convenient transportation, including the production of railroads. The economic boom enjoyed by western countries also enabled the rise of the skyscraper. These economic changes resulted in social changes that included a widened margin between the rich and poor. More germane to Stevenson's story are the breakout discovery of multiple personalities and a report from the Pall Mall Gazette on prostitution in London. In the late 1880s, the term "double consciousness" was coined after French doctors reported "a boy called Louis who had exhibited as many as five separate personalities.... Louis could jump between different mental ages or between states of abject hysteria, cunning criminality, and apparently normal boyhood at the appropriate trigger."[1] The wider fascination with psychic splitting coincided with Stevenson's writing of this, the first popular psychological thriller, a book that would open the door for the likes of Sir Arthur Conan Doyle and his famed Sherlock Holmes stories.

In July 1885, one year before *Dr. Jekyll and Mr. Hyde* was written, the *Pall Mall Gazette* published a report on child prostitution in London. As W.T. Stead, the editor, rummaged the streets, he "reported rumours of a monstrous libertine who 'may be said to be an absolute incarnation of brutal lust.... Here in London, moving about clad as respectably in broad cloth and fine linen as any bishop, with no foul shape or semblance of brute beast to mark him off from the rest of his fellows, is Dr —.'"[2] While it is unclear whether this report was the seed idea for Dr. Jekyll, it is clear that it awakened Victorian readers to the reality that "one might smile, and smile, and be a villain" (*Hamlet*, Act 5.1).

---

1. Roger Luckhurst, "Introduction" to *The Strange Case of Dr. Jekyll and Mr. Hyde and Other Tales*, by Robert Louis Stevenson (Oxford: OUP, 2008), xviii.
2. Luckhurst, xxv.

ABOUT THE AUTHOR

Robert Louis Stevenson, born in 1850, suffered for his entire life from a pulmonary lung disease which was never definitively diagnosed and that rendered him an invalid, dependent upon his parents for much of his life. The most formative period of Stevenson's life was his childhood, which he spent in his room, alone with books and his imagination, the fertile soil out of which sprang his most popular tales. Perhaps the combination of loving adventure coupled with the inability to *go* on adventure birthed his vigorous writing style and his adventure stories.

Despite his limitations, contrary to popular artistic leanings, he strove to thrill himself and he strove to thrill his readers. Nihilistic tales were popular in his days and artists of every kind posed as pessimists. "Stevenson seemed to say to the semi-suicides drooping round him at the cafe tables, drinking absinthe and discussing atheism: 'Hang it all... Painting pasteboard figures of pirates and admirals was better worth doing than all this, it was fun; it was fighting; it was a life and a lark; and if I can't do anything else, dang me but I will try to do that again!'"[3]

His stories swing wildly between pure adventure and rich philosophical allegory, but they all pay tribute to human desire and the often depraved nature of those desires. Perhaps this theme of human corruption was residual leftover from his parents' Calvinism which he exchanged for agnosticism. He rejected their theological and moral views in favor of a morally illicit lifestyle which he considered less hypocritical.

While Stevenson never believed in the Resurrection, Chesterton points out that Stevenson's stories repeatedly bear witness to the Fall. "We say lightly enough of a good man that he is a Christian without knowing it. But Stevenson was a Christian theologian without knowing it."[4] He traveled extensively—sometimes carried on a litter if needed—through Europe and even to America, where he married his wife (Fanny), always searching for a place to simultaneously relieve his pulmonary pain and feed his love for adventure.

All evidence suggests that he found relief on the islands of Samoa, which he described as the Islands of the Blest. He died quite suddenly when he was forty-four and was remembered fondly by the islanders as *Tusitala*, or the

---

3. G.K. Chesterton, *Robert Louis Stevenson* (Miami, FL: HardPress Publishers, 2013), np.
4. Ibid.

Teller of Tales. He wrote his own epitaph, which can be seen on his grave:

> Under the wide and starry sky
>> Dig the grave and let me lie:
> Glad did I live and gladly die,
>> And I laid me down with a will.
>
> This be the verse you 'grave for me:
>> *Here he lies where he long'd to be;*
> *Home is the sailor, home from the sea,*
>> *And the hunter home from the hill.*

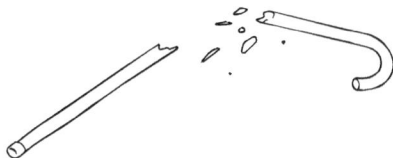

THE STORY BEHIND THE STORY

While the narrative of *Dr. Jekyll and Mr. Hyde* is intriguing, the story behind the story is equally fascinating, although elements of it are debated by scholars.

In 1824, James Hogg wrote *Confessions of a Justified Sinner* in which the protagonist, Wringham, "is accused of an escalating series of heinous crimes that he ascribes to Gil-Martin, an intimate friend who begins to take over his life, his physical likeness, and eventually his mind. In terms echoed by Jekyll's confession, Wringham agonizes that, "I was a being incomprehensible to myself. Either I had a second self . . . or else my body was at times possessed by a spirit over which it had no control."[5] Whether or not this story impacted Stevenson's imagination, we do not know, but the similarities are striking.

Stevenson once told a reporter that the story sprang from a dream: "All I dreamed about Dr. Jekyll was that

---

5. Luckhurst, xxi.

one man was being pressed into a cabinet, when he swallowed a drug and changed into another being. I awoke and said at once that I had found the missing link for which I had been looking so long, and before I again went to sleep almost every detail of the story, as it stands, was clear to me."[6]

He wrote feverishly for three days, demanding that he not be bothered unless the house was burning down. After he finished, he read his prized story to Fanny, his wife, who was not impressed. She felt that he had written a mere thriller and missed the thematic and allegorical potential in the story that would ultimately make it a classic. Legend has it that Stevenson was furious and, according to rather dubious reports, threw the entire manuscript in the fire.

He started from scratch and wrote "sixty-four thousand words in six days; more than ten thousand words a day."[7] That was ten times what most authors set as their quota, including the likes of Jack London and Ray Bradbury, but the miraculous nature of his productivity is even greater when we consider Fanny's testimony: "That an invalid in my husband's condition of health should have been able to perform the manual alone ... seems incredible. He was suffering from continual hemorrhages, and was hardly

---

6. Luckhurst, xi.

7. *Strange Case of Dr. Jekyll and Mr. Hyde*, ed. Martin A. Danahay (Toronto, Ontario: Broadview Editions, 2015), 132.

allowed to speak, his conversation usually being carried on by means of a slate and pencil."[8]

Stevenson astonished the world with not just the narrative itself, but with the kind of narrative he produced. *Dr. Jekyll and Mr. Hyde* is the genesis of a new genre, the psychological thriller. While common in books and films today, it was the first time that the real mystery of a story focused on the conflict *inside* a character. Before Stevenson, the best stories always had an internal conflict, but external forces played upon that internal conflict. In the case of Dr. Jekyll, this relationship is flipped and the internal conflict unleashes external conflicts. This genre is rife with complications, not least of which is the tendency for the main story (external conflict) to get muddied by the psychological story. It is easy for an author in this genre to confuse the reader at times, getting too clever with juggling so many layers of narrative. This confusion does happen in *Dr. Jeykll and Mr. Hyde*, but we can forgive Stevenson since he was breaking ground on a new genre.

As an interesting aside, Stevenson suggested that Jekyll be pronounced "Jee-kill," not "Jek-ill." He said that "Jekyll is a very good family name in England, and over there it is pronounced in the manner stated."[9]

---

8. Ian Bell, *Dreams of Exile: Robert Louis Stevenson, a Biography* (New York: Henry Hold, 1992), 174.

9. Mehew Ernest, "Letter to the Times," Nov. 28, 1980, Futility Closet, http://www.futilitycloset.com/2012/11/01/noted-7/ (accessed on January 31, 2017).

PLOT SUMMARY, SETTING, AND CHARACTERS

- *Setting:* London, England, in the late 1800s
- *Dr. Henry Jekyll:* a respected and mild-mannered physician.
- *Mr. Hyde:* a remorseless little man bent on violence and his own pleasure; the alter-ego of Dr. Jekyll, who transforms into Mr. Hyde after taking a serum
- *Gabriel John Utterson:* the primary narrator, a lawyer who is Dr. Jekyll's friend
- *Richard Enfield:* Utterson's distant cousin and regular companion who witnesses Hyde's first public violence
- *Hastie Lanyon:* longtime friend to Dr. Jekyll, a physician who first discovers Hyde's true identity
- *Mr. Poole:* Dr. Jekyll's butler

- *Sir Danvers Carew*: a kind old man and member of Parliament who is murdered by Hyde
- *Inspector Newcomen:* a policeman who joins Utterson to investigate the murder of Danvers Carew

The story begins with two friends, Mr. Utterson and Richard Enfield, walking past a house door that has no bell and no knocker and which triggers Enfield's memory of a horrible event that he witnessed one night just outside that very door. He tells Utterson that he saw a man run into a little girl and knock her down. What was worse, the man kept walking, trampling right over the girl. Onlookers were outraged at the act and at the unspeakably deformed appearance of the man named Hyde. He was brought to account and promised to pay a fine. Hyde entered at that knocker-less door and came out with a check signed not by Mr. Hyde, but by the upstanding doctor, Henry Jekyll. Utterson knows that the door serves as a back entrance to the home of their friend, Dr. Jekyll.

Knowing that Dr. Jekyll has willed all of his estate to Edward Hyde upon Jekyll's death or three-month disappearance, Gabriel Utterson suspects that Dr. Jekyll is being blackmailed by Hyde. Utterson discovers from Jekyll's butler that Hyde only uses the laboratory at the back of the house. Several weeks later, Dr. Jekyll hosts a party at which he assures Utterson that Hyde does not have any kind of hold on Jekyll.

One year later, Sir Danvers Carew is brutally murdered by Hyde who bludgeons his victim with a cane that Utterson once gave to Dr. Jekyll. Utterson leads the detective to Hyde's abode which they find ransacked and with Hyde long gone. Utterson visits Dr. Jekyll that afternoon and finds him anxious and sickly. Jekyll assures Utterson that Hyde is in hiding and will never be discovered.

For two months, Jekyll returns to his sociable self before suddenly shutting himself off from everyone, including Utterson, who seeks out their mutual friend, Dr. Lanyon. Lanyon is deeply disturbed by something related to Jekyll, but will not tell Utterson, though Lanyon does predict his own coming demise. Lanyon dies within two weeks, just before sending Utterson a letter with directions not to open it until Jekyll disappears or dies.

Shortly thereafter, an alarmed Poole drags Utterson to Jekyll's home, suspecting foul play. Afraid that Jekyll has been killed, they use an axe to break down the laboratory door and discover Hyde's body on the floor, apparently dead by poison. They note that he is wearing Jekyll's clothing and they search the laboratory, but cannot find any sign of Dr. Jekyll. On Jekyll's desk, they find an envelope addressed to Utterson. It contains a will with Hyde's name replaced by Utterson, a sealed packet, and a note instructing Utterson to read the letter that Lanyon previously gave him.

Lanyon's letter details a shocking encounter in which Lanyon witnessed the transformation of Hyde into Dr.

Jekyll, simply by drinking a chemical mixture. Lanyon closes the letter with the warning that what Jekyll shared afterward was much too horrifying to repeat.

The final chapter of the book is a full confession written by Jekyll, in which he describes his interest in the dual nature of man—the socially respectable coexisting with darker desires—and his scientific attempts to separate the two sides. He experimented on himself and found that his transformed self, which he named Edward Hyde, was both smaller and stronger than his regular self. As Edward Hyde, he felt pleasure and liberation. Jekyll dabbled with gratifying these darker desires for some time until one day he simply awoke transformed involuntarily. Transforming back into Jekyll grew progressively more difficult as Hyde grew more powerful. When he realized that he would soon permanently become Hyde, Jekyll made one last-ditch effort to hold off the transformation long enough to write a confession and inform the world of Hyde's (and his) true nature.

He suspects that Hyde will either kill himself or be hanged for his crimes, but he closes his letter convinced that Henry Jekyll will be no more.

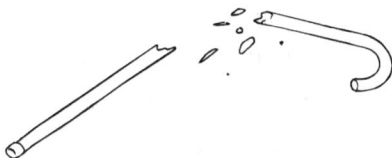

WORLDVIEW ANALYSIS

I still remember the spreading cultural shock in the late 80s when we learned that a man named Ted (such a harmless, regular, vanilla name) confessed to thirty brutal homicides which he committed in seven states over a four-year period. Ted Bundy was an all-American nice guy; in fact, the Mormon missionary who baptized Bundy said he was the type of guy you would want dating your sister, and while Bundy was on trial, his mother told the media, "He's my pride and joy. He wouldn't do anything wrong. We've always been proud of him. He's the kind of a son who never forgot Mother's Day."[10] Who would know a son better than his mother? And how could it be possible for a guy who never forgot Mother's Day to be a serial killer?

---

10. Stephen C. Smith, "Momma's Boy to Murderer: Saga of Ted Bundy," *Lakeland Ledger*, August 19, 1979.

None of us actually wanted to face the fact that we are, like Ted, capable of gross sin, so we wrote him off as a wacko. We decided that he was an outlier—a pedestrian version of Hitler, with a bad circuit breaker in his head. We conveniently leveraged his heinous crimes to defend our own not-so-badness: "I'm not perfect, but I'm no Bundy." For our present purposes, we might as well have said, "I'm a sinner, but at least I'm no Mr. Hyde."

Our comments were a convenient ploy to keep the reality of our sinful nature at bay. Ted did not make it easy on us. He said, "well-meaning, decent people will condemn the behavior of a Ted Bundy, while they're walking past a magazine rack full of the very kinds of things that send young kids down the road to be Ted Bundys."[11] He was convinced, and I think correctly, that a pornographic culture like ours is an incubator for monsters despite its best efforts to hide behind a shiny veneer. Our culture tell us to be pious, dutifully appearing to meet social norms.

With or without a respectable piety, God is unambiguous about the corruption of the human heart: "The heart is deceitful above all things, and desperately wicked; who can know it?" (Jeremiah 17:9). Paul declares in Romans 3:23, "All have sinned and fall short of the glory of God." For this reason, Paul agonized that "in me (that is, in my flesh) nothing good dwells; for to will is present with me,

---

11   "Psychopath Ted Bundy's Interview Before Execution," YouTube video, January 23, 1989, posted by "Zeke Reloaded," accessed on June 12, 2017, https://www.youtube.com/watch?v=hVyhKgd9_No..

but how to perform what is good I do not find. For the good that I will to do, I do not do; but the evil I will not to do, that I practice. Now if I do what I will not to do, it is no longer I who do it, but sin that dwells in me" (Rom. 7:18-20). Stevenson echoed this mystery when he wrote, "It follows that man is twofold at least; that he is not a rounded and autonomous empire; but that in the same body with him there dwell other powers tributary but independent."[12]

Dr. Jekyll is the everyman, suffering the common lot of humanity. None of us is immune to the heart's corrupt nature and each of us "is tempted when he is drawn away by his own desires and enticed. Then, when desire has conceived, it gives birth to sin; and sin, when it is full-grown, brings forth death" (Jas. 1:14-15). A "good man" and a "bad man" share the same systemic corruption. Only God's grace keeps them both from succumbing to the rapacious appetites of Hell. Indeed, Jonathan Edwards, writing one hundred years before Dr. Jekyll came on stage, said "if it were not for the restraining hand of God upon them, they would soon break out, they would flame out after the same manner, as the same corruptions, the same enmity does in the hearts of damned souls."[13]

---

12. Claire Harman, *Myself and the Other Fellow: A Life of Robert Louis Stevenson* (New York: HarperCollins, 2005), 167.
13. Jonathan Edwards, *Sinners in the Hands of an Angry God: A Casebook*, ed. Wilson H. Kimnach, Caleb J.D. Maskell, and Kenneth P. Minkema (New Haven, CT: Yale University, 2010), 37.

Every one of us, whether Ted Bundy or Miss Goody-Goody, is alienated from God and suffers from the disintegration of the person caused by sin. The old man living in us (Rom. 6:6-10) will not be stifled, and we rightly fear he will reveal himself. We feel shame for our natural leanings, but our fear of being discovered magnifies the shame ten-fold. Like Dr. Jekyll, we cover our proclivities with lies and shams, with posturing and preening, and we are rarely honest enough with God or with ourselves to confess the truth and seek the healing that can only come by the blood of Christ.

The universal fallenness of man is a reality, whether in a prudish culture like the Victorian, or a pornographic one like our own. The great enigma that Stevenson offers the Victorians and us is Dr. Jekyll, a man who appears virtuous, but who is corrupt where it matters most in his heart.

The view that Victorians were prudish and repressive is a generalization and exceptions abound, but there is no doubt that the upper class valued external piety. Dr. Jekyll was the prototypical Victorian gentleman: well-mannered, well-dressed, well-polished. Stevenson's story hit where it hurt, reminding Victorian pietists (whether Stevenson meant to or not) that people are corrupt and cannot heal themselves by simple will-power.

This reality is true for individuals and for the societies comprised by those individuals. For example, the industrial revolution that came just prior to the Victorian period afforded more wealth and power to the Victorian elite, but that progress increased abuses of women and children that were largely ignored. High society thrived with all the appearance of modesty and sobriety and leisure while unnumbered societal ills went unaddressed. The problem was not the industrial advances per se, but the corrupt human heart. While education and legislation certainly helped eliminate some of these abuses, these ills still haunt us in both developed and undeveloped countries. This is because neither knowledge nor force is sufficient to heal what ails us. Dr. Jekyll acts as a mirror to a society so bent on appearances, and a reminder to all citizens of the corruption that lurks beneath the surface of the human heart.

Flannery O'Connor once wrote, "to the hard of hearing you shout, and for the almost blind you draw large and startling figures."[14] To a people growing more practiced at an external show of goodness (like the Victorians) or intent on sexually liberating humanity from the restrictive and outdated moral codes of monotheism (like us), Dr. Jekyll is a large and startling reminder of human corruption.

Sin has a powerful gravitational drag on the human heart, and fighting that pull demands a supernatural power. Jekyll was an ordinary secret sinner who indulged his dark desires in small doses, succumbing slowly to that gravitational force without realizing the cumulative effect

---

14. Flannery O'Connor, *Mystery and Manners* (New York: Farrar, Straus and Giroux, 1970), 13.

on the soul.[15] He invested his energies in the pleasures of sin until they were too strong for him to overcome by his own power. The monster he became was quite different from the gentleman he once was, but the latent potential for that monster was always inside his heart. Like a seed, it only wanted germination.

As with Bundy's finally exposed brutality, we find it easy to condemn Mr. Hyde's violence, and we should. God's word is clear regarding such overt sin: "Therefore put to death your members which are on the earth: fornication, uncleanness, passion, evil desire, covetousness, which is idolatry" (Col. 3:5). And Ephesians 4:17-19 says, "no longer walk as the rest of the Gentiles walk, in the futility of their mind, having their understanding darkened, being alienated from the life of God, because of the ignorance that is in them, because of the blindness of their heart; who, being past feeling, have given themselves over to lewdness, to work all uncleanness with greediness."

Undoubtedly, Bundy and Hyde were "past feeling" and gave themselves over to work all uncleanness, but one does not become a Ted Bundy or Edward Hyde overnight. For this very reason, the drawn arrow of God's judgment in history and in the Bible is not pointed toward overt sinners like them, but toward posers and preeners.

The real culprit of this story is not Mr. Hyde, but Dr. Jekyll. Paul, following Christ's lead, bent his fury not toward the Hydes of the world, but towards the Dr. Jekylls,

---

15. Davidson, 73.

who worked overtime to cover their hearts' leprosy while secretly indulging in "small" sins. Dr. Jekyll is the one we should most fear, and he is the one most like us.

As one author put it, "When St. Paul attacks the 'natural man' (I Cor. 2:14) he is not taking on all the drug addicts, winos, and hookers of Corinth. Rather, he is referring to man at his best—yachtsman, advisor to kings and presidents, philosopher, harpsichord player, and war hero. *That* was the man who did not 'know God' (1 Cor. 1:21). St. Paul was taking on the Corinthian aristocracy."[16] Something very similar is, indeed, happening in *Dr. Jekyll and Mr. Hyde*. Stevenson paints a startling portrait in the character of Dr. Jekyll, a character whose growing corruption hides beneath a refined appearance.

Dr. Jekyll himself says that the restrictions of social proprieties birthed in him a profound duplicity: "I concealed my pleasures; and when I reached years of reflection, and began to look round me and take stock of my progress and position in the world, I stood already committed to a profound duplicity of life. Many a man would have even blazoned such irregularities as I was guilty of; but from the high views that I had set before me, I regarded and hid them with an almost morbid sense of shame."

For this reason, many critics, professional and armchair alike, believe that Dr. Jekyll's main ill is sexual repression, both heterosexual and homosexual. They suggest that

16. Douglas Wilson, "Beowulf: The UnChrist," in *Beowulf: A New Verse Rendering* (Moscow, ID: Canon Press, 2013), 114.

Hyde, his alter-ego, is a voluptuary free to roam in the fields of sexual liberation against the repressive Victorian morals that would force him to suffer beneath the lash of sexual tension—as if sex is the only cause of duplicity and, therefore, shame. Stevenson, interestingly enough, was disappointed by this interpretation and said so: "There is no harm in a voluptuary, no harm whatever—in what prurient fools call immorality. ... [Hyde was] no more sensual than another."[17] Perhaps he found *this* reading of his story too simplistic, and he wanted Dr. Jekyll's struggle to include the full gamut of sinful possibilities.

Jekyll, like Hamlet, is an arrant knave crawling between earth and heaven (*Hamlet*, Act 3.1), torn between a desire to be good by one's own effort and the strong downward pull of lust. When Hamlet said, "I could accuse me of such things, that it were better my mother had not borne me," he dares admit what Jekyll will not.

Unlike Hamlet, however, Dr. Jekyll has no one to blame for his troubles. Jekyll admits to being born wealthy and healthy, having nothing to impinge on his happiness. His sinful indulgence has nothing to do with circumstances and everything to do with the pleasure of sin. As Augustine wrote, "We have an inordinate preference for these goods of a lower order and neglect the better and the higher good.[18] In describing the overwhelming power of

---

17. Bell, 193.

18. Augustine, *Confessions*, trans. Alber C. Outler (Peabody, MA: Hendrickson Publishers, 2004), 31 [2.5].

sin in his life, Augustine said that "the thorn bushes of lust grew rank about my head, and there was no hand to root them out."[19] As it was with Augustine, so it was with Jekyll. The key difference between the two men is that Augustine broke under the power of Christ's forgiveness, and Dr. Jekyll broke under the power of sin.

In this respect, Dr. Jekyll is no less guilty than Mr. Hyde because they are the same man. As 1+1=2, so the vigorous, surging, feral Hyde is simply the product of Dr. Jekyll plus self-indulgence. Many of us are under the illusion that we can privately indulge our base desires in small doses. This illusion is pervasive in a world grown comfortable with the internet. The ready availability of free pornography is a cheap thrill, and there are millions of Jekylls in the world who keep feeding their sinful nature without realizing that it will ultimately break out in unexpected places, causing surprising damage.

Whether a person indulges in lusts privately or not, every person needs the forgiveness granted through Christ, and every person needs the power of the Holy Spirit to combat the old man of sin within. Paul Tournier makes it quite clear that no one is free from a very real guilt for sin:

> Before Jesus there are not two opposed human categories, the guilty and the righteous; there are only the guilty—the woman to whom Jesus speaks God's pardon [Jn. 8:3-11], and the men who will receive it in their turn, since by their silent withdrawal they

19. Ibid., 28 [2.3].

admit their own guilt...To offer grace only is to cut
off half the Gospel. Grace is for the woman trem-
bling at her guilt. But her accusers will be able to
find grace only by rediscovering for themselves the
shudder of guilt. On the other hand, to present only
the sternness of God also cuts off half the Gospel.
Jesus does not awaken guilt in order to condemn,
but to save, for grace is given to him who humbles
himself, and becomes aware of his guilt. [20]

Dr. Jekyll actually embarked on experimentation because he wanted to avoid the consequences of self-indulgence and hoped that he could live a dichotomy, blaming
Hyde for any damage. He saw avoidance, not repentance,
as the solution to guilt, but he could not avoid that guilt
altogether. After Hyde killed Sir Danvers Carew, for example, Dr. Jekyll momentarily buckled under severe guilt.
He tried to be good within his own power, but could not
sustain the fight. Whether we call it a sense of guilt or
whether we call it conscience, "the point of the story is not
that a man can cut himself off from his conscience, but
that he cannot. The surgical operation is fatal in the story.
It is an amputation of which both the parts die." [21]

The fact that Dr. Jekyll is a physician is a profound
irony. He may be a competent doctor (although this fact
seems completely besides the point to Stevenson), but his
competence is no protection against the kind of sickness
that he suffers. The healer cannot heal himself, and all his

---

20. *Guilt and Grace* (New York: Harper and Row, 1962), 112.
21. Chesterton, np.

efforts to heal look very much like a deeper sickness. Dr. Jekyll is a poor physician for himself, bent and broken by sin, and suffering from a growing inner disintegration. What he needs, but cannot find, is repentance, a change of heart born from regret and sorrow that leads to a change of life. Instead, he dances with the devilish lusts within and, according to Chesterton, the moral of the story is "that the devil is a liar, and more especially a traitor; that he is more dangerous to his friends than his foes."[22] Or, to put it another way, "Everybody, soon or late, sits down to a banquet of consequences."[23]

The story accurately paints a complicated picture at moral, psychological, and social levels. Whether Dr. Jekyll falls prey to common human lusts or whether he suffers from a more complex case of dissociative identity disorder, the problem remains unresolved. The layered intricacies and subtle nuances of the human mind and heart require more than a paint-by-numbers application of truth and grace. A story like *Dr. Jekyll and Mr. Hyde*, written as it is by an agnostic, can only offer the problem. God alone offers solutions. Perhaps Chesterton's interpretation of the story as a simple analogy for man's sinful nature is somewhat simplistic (as some allege), but Stevenson cannot offer Dr. Jekyll anything like the solution God offers to those who feed the flesh and slowly sear their conscience.

---

22. Ibid.

23. This saying is popularly attributed to Stevenson (in fact it is somewhat adapted from his original).

When Stevenson points us to the dual nature of the human heart and ends the story, Christian readers should recognize the missing cure: Christ's atonement: "There is one God, and there is one mediator between God and men, the man Christ Jesus, who gave himself as a ransom for all" (1 Tim. 2:5-6 ESV). "For Christ also suffered once for sins, the righteous for the unrighteous, that he might bring us to God, being put to death in the flesh but made alive in the spirit" (1 Peter 3:18 ESV). *Dr. Jekyll and Mr. Hyde* shouldn't be read as "just" a simple morality tale, but it certainly has important lessons for those who care about Christ's kingdom and his bride, the church.

First, for Christians, the same self-love, self-reliance, and desire for autonomy that finally consumes Dr. Jekyll lurks inside every last one of us. All have sinned, all have gone astray, and our sin must be confessed both horizontally (to those against whom we have sinned) and vertically (to the God who is holy and sent his son to die as atonement for our sins).

Second, the consequences for individuals who refuse to confess are dire and the consequences for cultures that foster posturing, deceit, and defensiveness are equally so. In a spiritual sense, a person who will not confess his sin and lean on Christ will perish. That same spiritual death happens to a culture that is embarrassed by the admission of weakness or sin or dependence. That culture may rise to a kind of power on its own wings, but its spiritual death ultimately results in a physical death. History is littered with those ruins.

Third, the church is not immune to these dangers. She too is comprised of people whose proclivity to hide their sin and appear holy is undeniable. It is not difficult to find congregations full of Dr. Jekylls, no matter the denomination, but the church must foster a culture in which dependence on confession of sin is a sign of maturity, not a social stigma. Christ came for those who recognize their sin, confess it, and acknowledge their need for a savior. Mature Christians are those who neither wallow in their own worminess (they confess and move on) nor promote the appearance of personal piety (they confess and live humbly). The church should overflow with those who gladly lift their eyes away from themselves to gaze upon Jesus Christ and who flee a life of posturing so vividly displayed by Dr. Jekyll. God is in the business of bringing about a coherence of the soul and, thereby, a cultural coherence. He knows the power of confession to reshape the soul and form this coherence, so he confronts us so that we will no longer hide our real nature from him or from ourselves.

Bundy and Jekyll are both sinners, guilty by nature. God's warning is equally strong to each: He who will not confess his sins and repent commits spiritual suicide. He who will not turn and run toward Christ will run headlong into self-destruction, "for he who sows to his flesh will of the flesh reap corruption, but he who sows to the Spirit will of the Spirit reap everlasting life" (Galatians

6:8). *The Strange Case of Dr. Jekyll and Mr. Hyde* illustrates the first half of this truth better than most.

QUOTABLES

1. "Mr. Hyde was pale and dwarfish, he gave an impression of deformity without any nameable malformation."
    ~ Chapter 2, "Search for Mr. Hyde"

2. "Just to put your good heart at rest, I will tell you one thing: the moment I choose, I can be rid of Mr. Hyde."
    ~ Chapter 3, "Dr. Jekyll Was Quite at Ease"

3. "Mr. Hyde broke out of all bounds and clubbed him to the earth. And next moment, with ape-like fury, he was trampling his victim under foot and hailing down a storm of blows, under which the bones were audibly shattered and the body jumped upon the roadway."
    ~ Chapter 4, "The Carew Murder Case"

4. "He could have wished it otherwise; never in his life had he been conscious of so sharp a wish to see and touch his fellow-creatures; for struggle as he might,

there was borne in upon his mind a crushing anticipa-
tion of calamity."

~ Chapter 8, "The Last Night"

5. "Poole nodded. 'Once,' he said. 'Once I heard it weep-
    ing!' 'Weeping? how's that?' said the lawyer, conscious
    of a sudden chill of horror. 'Weeping like a woman or a
    lost soul,' said the butler."

    ~ Chapter 8, "The Last Night"

6. "I thus drew steadily nearer to that truth, by whose
    partial discovery I have been doomed to such a dreadful
    shipwreck: that man is not truly one, but truly two."

    ~ Chapter 10, "Full Statement of the Case"

7. "Jekyll had more than a father's interest; Hyde had
    more than a son's indifference."

    ~ Chapter 10, "Full Statement of the Case"

8. "Yes, I had gone to bed Henry Jekyll, I had awakened
    Edward Hyde."

    ~ Chapter 10, "Full Statement of the Case"

9. "I was slowly losing hold of my original and better self,
    and becoming slowly incorporated with my second and
    worse."

    ~ Chapter 10, "Full Statement of the Case"

10. "My devil had been long caged, he came out roaring."

    ~ Chapter 10, "Full Statement of the Case"

11. "It was in my own person that I was once more tempted to trifle with my conscience; and it was as an ordinary secret sinner that I at last fell before the assaults of temptation."

    ~ Chapter 10, "Full Statement of the Case"

21 SIGNIFICANT QUESTIONS AND ANSWERS

1. Why is it so important that Stevenson set his story of a monster in an urban setting populated by professional and reputable men?

   > The contrast created by a monster hiding amongst wine connoisseurs and gentlemen is all the more striking. Setting it in contemporary Victorian period augments the contrast and gives the story a kind of prophetic voice in the wider culture, a voice that speaks out against the various two-faced expressions of human nature so common in civilized countries.

2. If Jesus sat down for a meal with Dr. Jekyll, what would Jesus say to him? What are some passages where Jesus warns against merely external righteousness?

   > Dr. Jekyll, you make the outside of the cup and dish clean, but your inward part is full of greed and

wickedness (Lk. 11:39). Woe to you, for you cleanse
the outside of the cup and dish, but inside they are
full of extortion and self-indulgence. Blind Pharisee,
first cleanse the inside of the cup and dish, that the
outside of them may be clean also (Matt. 23:25-26).
You are like those who justify themselves before men,
but God knows your heart; for that which is highly
esteemed among men is detestable in the sight of
God (Lk. 16:15).

3. Consider other verses that address Dr. Jekyll in any way.
    There are many options.

    "All we like sheep have gone astray; we have turned,
    every one, to his own way; and the Lord has laid on
    Him the iniquity of us all" (Is. 53:6).

    "The heart is deceitful above all things, and desper-
    ately sick; who can understand it? I the Lord search
    the heart and test the mind, to give every man
    according to his ways, according to the fruit of his
    deeds" (Jer. 17:9-10 ESV).

    "Counsel in the heart of man is like deep water,
    but a man of understanding will draw it out" (Prov.
    20:5).

4. William Law said, "Self is the root, the tree, and the branches of all the evils of our fallen state," and George MacDonald said, "a man must be set free from the sin he is, which makes him do the sin he does." How does *Dr. Jekyll and Mr. Hyde* reinforce those statements?

> As G.K. Chesterton put it, the story's shock value is not that one man is actually two, but that two men are actually one. The real shock to our modern sensibilities is that such distinctly different men are inextricably bound up in one very nice man. Dr. Jekyll's self, his heart, is the root, the tree, and the branches of all the evils which Hyde lives out. Our selves, our inmost person, will come out our fingertips. We ultimately do what we are.

5. If this story were released today for the first time, would it sell as quickly or have as big an impact as it did originally?

> The novel is unlikely to have the same act now, since it predated all of Freud's psychoanalytical theories, it helped create what we call the thriller and mystery genres, and it came out during a time of great humanistic optimism about the moral strength of humanity. Furthermore, that moral optimism was beginning to crumble with reports of widespread abuses and gristly murders (like Jack the Ripper) committed in the seedier parts of London.
>
> Perhaps, too, there was still a residual biblical imprint on the cultural psyche which has largely faded.

A post-Christian culture lacks the nutrients in the soil required to make sound use of an allegory like this one. We would find it interesting, perhaps a thriller, and nothing more.

6.   One critic wrote, "We would welcome a spectre, a ghoul, or even a vampire gladly, rather than meet Mr. Edward Hyde."[24] In what ways is he correct?

One possible answer is that a ghost or a monster might frighten, but it also prompts a fight. According to legend, there are ways to defeat a vampire, however much it scares us witless. There are ways to survive a zombie apocalypse; ghosts, ghouls, and vampires are *other* while Hyde is the *self*. Witnesses to Hyde's violence are nearly paralyzed by the spectacle. He is not monster enough, not *other* enough. He is us, but not us. While people's sensibilities are shocked by him, no one tries to kill him because they're not sure what to do. They can't even quite define what is wrong with him.

7.   What did the Samoan people call Robert Louis Stevenson?

Tusitala, or the "Teller of Tales."

---

24   "R. Stevenson's New Story," *The Saturday Review*, January 9, 1886, 55-56.

8. What did the *Pall Mall Gazette* report one year prior to
    the publication of *Dr. Jekyll and Mr. Hyde* which may
    have planted a seed in Stevenson's imagination?

    > Answers will vary, but should have pertinent
    > details. W.T. Stead, the editor, heard reports of a
    > fiend who "may be said to be an absolute incar-
    > nation of brutal lust.... Here in London, moving
    > about clad as respectably in broad cloth and fine
    > linen as any bishop, with no foul shape or sem-
    > blance of brute beast to mark him off from the rest
    > of his fellows, is Dr —."

9. What kept Stevenson bedridden with his books and
    imagination during his childhood?

    > A pulmonary disease that was never definitively
    > diagnosed.

10. In his "Memoirs of Himself," Stevenson wrote, "It is
    told of me that I came once to my mother with these
    words: 'Mama, I have drawed a man's body; shall I draw
    his soul now?'" Did he successfully draw a man's soul in
    this novel?

    > All great authors know that a character's soul is
    > shown by what he desires and by what he does to
    > attain that object. Dr. Jekyll's pursuit of a dual life
    > as respectable physician by day and dissolute rogue
    > by night betrays the caliber of his soul. Because they
    > go unrepented, his lusts ultimately win the day and

he sells his soul for unbridled pleasure. So yes, he
did draw a soul.

11. What do Utterson and Enfield see that triggers
Enfield's memory of his first encounter with Hyde and
why is it symbolically interesting?

> A knockerless door which serves as a back entrance
> to Jekyll's house, literally showing Dr. Jekyll's desire
> for isolation and symbolically showing the hidden
> nature of his sins.

12. What is Hyde's first criminal act?

> He murders Sir Danvers Carew.

13. What does Lanyon witness that ultimately kills him
with fright? Does Lanyon's death signify anything
important regarding the impact of Dr. Jekyll's sin?

> Lanyon witnesses the transformation of Hyde back
> into Dr. Jekyll. Lanyon's death is evidence that Dr.
> Jekyll's "private" sins are destroying his relationships,
> both figuratively and literally.

14. In his confession, Dr. Jekyll wrote, "I felt younger, light-
er, happier in body; within I was conscious of a heady
recklessness, a current of disordered sensual images
running like a millrace in my fancy, a solution of the
bonds of obligation, an unknown but not an innocent
freedom of the soul. I knew myself, at the first breath of

this new life, to be more wicked, tenfold more wicked, sold a slave to my original evil; and the thought, in that moment, braced and delighted me like wine" (64). How does his confession mirror our modern desires?

> He reinforces the modern longing for liberation from moral self-restraint. The sexual liberation prefers to live without moral constraint and calls it honesty, as if giving in to sin is the only way to live authentically. Authenticity is, no doubt, important and a basic biblical principle as shown by the way Christ derided pharisaical hypocrisy; however, Christ calls sinners to pursue integrity by *honestly* confessing sin to God and to those against whom we sin. He calls us to live uprightly by the power of the Holy Spirit.

15. In what ways is Dr. Jekyll representative of humanity?

> Answers will vary, but should touch on Dr. Jekyll's lust for power, hunger for admiration while simultaneously engaging in immorality, and ultimate pursuit of self.

16. What is one consequence for a society that values piety instead of repentance as the status quo?

> Individuals in that society will unsuccessfully repress their lusts until those lusts break out violently.

17. Are there any clear Christians in the novel?

> There are several characters who are pietistic and
> who deeply value the status quo, but none are clear
> Christians. While they might be accused of mild
> hypocrisy, only Dr. Jekyll is guilty of wild hypocrisy.

18. Does your home life foster a culture of confession or
    is it a culture of posturing, deceit, and defensiveness?
    What are the indicators and what are some solutions?

> Answers will vary, but a home that humbly em-
> braces confession will do so both horizontally (to
> others) and vertically (to God). As a solution, one's
> confession always starts with one's own sins first
> (Matt. 7:3).

19. In what ways is America a society of Dr. Jekylls? Is
    there hope for change? What can you do concretely
    that might change larger society?

> Answers will again vary, but our celebrity culture is
> evidence of this Jekyll fakery. A tendency to make
> changes as political activists should be tempered by
> the reminder of how God loves to work in ordinary
> people with ordinary relationships, like parents and
> children.

20. In your opinion, what is the cause for departure of youth from the church? Is it that they want to live the Dr. Jekyll and Mr. Hyde life or is it because they found the church populated by Dr. Jekylls?

     Answers will vary.

21. Read Stevenson's "A Portrait" and make any comparisons between the poem and the story of Dr. Jekyll and Mr. Hyde.

     A Portrait

       I am a kind of farthing dip,
       Unfriendly to the nose and eyes;
       A blue-behinded ape, I skip
       Upon the trees of Paradise.

       At mankind's feast, I take my place
       In solemn, sanctimonious state,
       And have the air of saying grace
       While I defile the dinner plate.

       I am the "smiler with the knife,"
       The battener upon garbage, I —
       Dear Heaven, with such a rancid life,
       Were it not better far to die?

       Yet still, about the human pale,
       I love to scamper, love to race,
       To swing by my irreverent tail
       All over the most holy place;

And when at length, some golden day,
The unfailing sportsman, aiming at
Shall bag, me—all the world shall say
Thank God, and there's an end of that!

Notice certain descriptions of himself that would be
fitting for either Jekyll or Hyde:

- "a blue-behinded ape" (Hyde)
- "I take my place in solemn, sanctimonious state,
  and have the air of saying grace while I defile
  the dinner plate" (Jekyll)
- "I am the smiler with the knife" (Hyde)
- "The battener upon garbage, I" (Jekyll)
- "With such a rancid life, were it not better far
  to die?" (Jekyll and Hyde)
- "Swing by my irreverent tail all over the most
  holy place" (Hyde)

FURTHER DISCUSSION AND REVIEW

The following review will help you master your reading.

CHARACTERS

Be able to compare and contrast Jekyll and Hyde (including their mannerisms, weaknesses, and strengths). Be able to suggest reasons why Utterson is the appropriate narrator of this story. Also, be able to contrast Utterson and Jekyll, especially their responses to evil.

SETTING

Be able to describe the atmosphere of the setting and how it impacts the characters and mirrors the pivotal moments of conflict in the story.

PLOT

Be able to map the narrative arc of the story, including the key conflicts along the way, and describe specific moments that make Jekyll's moral collapse convincing. Be able to describe the use of flashbacks in the narrative.

CONFLICT

List the main characters and describe the tension between any and all of them. Then describe the inner conflict for each character.

PERSPECTIVE

Be able to explain possible reasons why Stevenson decided to write large portions of the story in first person (albeit from the perspective of several characters). How does that change the way a reader interacts with the story, themes, and characters?

THEME STATEMENTS

> Violence will break out in persons who belong to a society which values piety, not repentance, as the status quo.

> Humanism will either enslave us to lust or enslave us to moralism.

> The "freedom" of doing whatever you want is actually slavery.

> Searing one's conscience has a cumulative impact on the heart and mind.

Nobility is more than external; it is an internal state of the heart.

Greater courage is required when confronting internal conflicts than when confronting external conflicts.

Hypocrisy is the most destructive vice for an individual and for a society.

The consequence of hiding immorality is greater guilt and eventually spiritual suicide.

Stevenson goes to great length to use first person narrative voice (from several characters) throughout the book. The pronoun "I" becomes central to the story's message and reveals the complexity of individuals.

Now compose several more statement themes that you noticed in the reading not mentioned above. Start by looking at the various relationships in the story.

A NOTE FROM THE PUBLISHER:
TAKING THE CLASSICS QUIZ

Once you have finished the worldview guide, you can prepare for the end-of-book test. Each test will consist of a short-answer section on the book itself and the author, a short-answer section on plot and the narrative, and a long-answer essay section on worldview, conflict, and themes.

Each quiz, along with other helps, can be downloaded for free at www.canonpress.com/ClassicsQuizzes. If you have any questions about the quiz or its answers or the Worldview Guides in general, you can contact Canon Press at service@canonpress.com or 208.892.8074.

ABOUT THE AUTHOR

Ben Palpant has a Bachelor's Degree from Whitworth University and is a teacher at The Oaks Academy. He has written several books including *Sojourner Songs, Pepin and the Magician,* and *Tales For My Children,* an audiobook. His book *A Small Cup of Light* chronicles his experience of temporarily losing his ability to walk, speak, feed himself, and read. He lives in Spokane, Washington with his wife, Kirsten, and five children.

www.ingramcontent.com/pod-product-compliance
Lightning Source LLC
Chambersburg PA
CBHW071933020426
42331CB00010B/2846